Was This Heaven?

A Bur Oak Original

Was This

A Self-Portrait of Iowa on Early Postcards

A Selection of Postcards from the David A. Wilson Collection

Lyell D. Henry, Jr.

Heaven?

EVERY DAY IN REINBECK IOWA.

University of Iowa Press Ψ Iowa City

University of Iowa Press, Iowa City 52242
Printed in the United States of America

Design by Richard Hendel

The postcards on pages 70, 74, 88, 95, 108, 128, 140,
147, 148, 152, 169, 193, 215, 219, and 232 are
reproduced courtesy of the State Historical Society
of Iowa, Iowa City.

Printed on acid-free paper

Library of Congress Cataloging-in-Publication Data
Henry, Lyell D.
    Was this heaven? a self-portrait of Iowa on early
postcards / by Lyell D. Henry, Jr.
        p.   cm.—(A Bur oak original)
    Includes bibliographical references and index.
    ISBN 0-87745-520-1 (cloth)
    1. Iowa—Social life and customs—Pictorial
works.   2. Iowa—Pictorial works.   3. Postcards—
Iowa.   I. Title.   II. Series.
F622.H46   1995
977.7—dc20   95-17620
                                                      CIP

01 00 99 98 97 96 95 C 5 4 3 2 1

Contents

Preface, *vii*

Greetings from Iowa! *1*

1 Hawkeyes, *13*

2 The Kind We Raise, *47*

3 Everything's Up to Date in River City, *79*

4 How We Do Things, *115*

5 Booster Days, *149*

6 Big News, *173*

7 Keeping 'Em Down on the Farm, *195*

8 'Til the Boys Come Home, *237*

References, *251*

Index of Towns, *253*

Preface

The images in this book depict Iowa and Iowans during the years 1905 through 1919 and are taken from photographic postcards made in those years. Although I supplied a handful of these postcards from my own collection and obtained another fifteen from the collection of the State Historical Society of Iowa, most came from the collection of David A. Wilson of Waterloo, Iowa. So rich and ample is the Wilson collection that I often found it difficult to make choices and, very reluctantly, had to pass by at least as many superb postcards as I settled upon. Another person in my place could easily have made a quite different selection. I am confident, however, that the postcards chosen do represent accurately the flavor and subject matter found in a very large portion of those early photographic postcards.

In the captions accompanying the images, words enclosed in quotation marks are taken directly from inscriptions—sometimes the photographer's but usually the sender's—found on the postcards. It is often impossible to determine exactly the years of origin of photographic postcards, and since all in this book fall within such a brief period (in fact, most are confined to the even briefer span of 1905 through 1916), I have not specified actual or estimated dates in the captions. I do include the locations of the images whenever known. Principally concerned to find postcards that revealed interesting things about Iowans and everyday life in Iowa in the opening years of this century, I made no systematic effort to maximize the number of Iowa towns included in my selection or to achieve balance among regions of the state. However, the Index of Towns shows that, in fact, many towns are included and that all parts of the state have at least some representation.

In a very real sense, this is David A. Wilson's book as much as it is mine, because, in addition to providing most of the postcards used, he was indispensably engaged in the book from the start. David gave me unrestricted access to his collection, responded to my requests for specific kinds of postcards by digging into his collection and usually finding what I needed, and, throughout, was an invaluable source of information and advice. He not only made hundreds of photocopies of postcards for my use but allowed me to hold a very large number of his postcards at my house for more than a year while I worked on this book. He even let me send my final selection of postcards (not merely photographs of them) off to the printer, thus making it possible for the reproductions in this book to be taken directly from the postcards themselves. In short, I could never have completed—or even begun—this book without David's help and cooperation, both of which went far beyond what I could have reasonably expected. For these and all of his many acts of generosity and friendship, I offer here my most genuine thanks and dedicate this book to him.

I also wish to thank the State Historical Society of Iowa for permitting me to use postcard images in the Society's collection; Mary Bennett, the Society's photo archivist, for making the Society's collection available for my inspection and providing photocopies of hundreds of postcards; Charlotte Fallon and Elinor Day, two of my colleagues at Mount Mercy College, for providing critical readings of my manuscript; and Lorna Olson, for doing her usual fine job of getting my writing into error-free typed form.

Was This Heaven?

Greetings from Iowa!

With Kinnamon's Band Gowrie Ia.

During the dozen or so years immediately preceding the entry of the United States into World War I in 1917, a frenzy for sending and collecting picture postcards reached American shores by way of Europe and soon had hundreds of thousands of Americans in thrall. The craze was helped along by the U.S. Post Office, which from 1898 through 1901 had made several accommodating changes in postal regulations and postage rates. Swarms of entrepreneurs rushing in to tap all the money-making possibilities of the latest fad soon brought on an avalanche of domestically produced postcards. Not only the stupefying numbers but also the rich variety and generally high quality of these cards have caused collectors to hail these opening years of the twentieth century as the "golden age" of postcards.

Among the many types of postcards turned out during those boom years was the photographic card—that is, a postcard consisting of an actual photograph developed (in black-and-white or brown tones) on photographic paper cut to standard postcard size. Exploiting this segment of the new market was a large fraternity of professional photographers both widely and densely strewn throughout the nether regions of American society. Their ranks included practitioners of the conventional formal poses executed in the photographic studios of the cities and towns of America; specialists in the novelty shots taken at vacation resorts, fairs, and amusement parks; confectioners of whimsical tall-tale scenes depicting encounters with larger-than-life fish, gigantic hogs, or outsized ears of corn; and itinerants and free-lancers, who kept the postcard racks of innumerable small-town drugstores filled with pictures of Main Street, last spring's flood, the whistle-stop visit of President Taft, the new water tower, and other sights and wonders of local pride. Thanks to the commercial availability after 1902 of inexpensive and easy-to-operate cameras designed to produce negatives of postcard size, many amateurs, too, added to the Post Office's burden. From their hands came vast quantities of cards bearing highly personal pictorial fare, such as images of Uncle Bob, Baby Dora, or Fido, the new house or automobile, the annual family picnic, the Sunday school outing, and the Christmas tree in the parlor.

No region of the United States was immune to the postcard epidemic of the early twentieth century, and that it didn't spare Iowa is evident in the thousands of Iowa cards from the period which can still be found in postcard collections, antique shops, and family albums in the state today. The more than two hundred cards presented here offer a generous sample of the range of subject matter found on the early photographic postcards. The handful of postcards in chapter eight date from 1917 through 1919, but almost all of the remaining postcards originated in a very narrow time span—the dozen years reaching from 1905 through 1916. All of the images are of Iowa or Iowans, and doubtless, too, most of the photographers making the images were Iowans; both professionals and amateurs are amply represented.

Although most of the creators of these cards were obscure then and are unknown or forgotten today, they nonetheless often did work of very high technical and aesthetic merit, as many of the cards attest. What is especially likely to fetch viewers today, however, is the documentary character of the postcards, which pile up fascinating and beguiling glimpses of Iowa and its people at a time long past. Here are detailed depictions, for instance, of period clothing and hairstyles, of celebrations, ceremonies, and entertainments, of school, church, and social activities, of farms, city streets, and public buildings, and of the multitudinous ways of getting and spending and of making a living—an amazingly rich visual record of everyday life and its setting in Iowa when this century was very young.

To be sure, this postcard record is selective. Were there, for instance, no run-down houses, seedy businesses, malnourished children, squalid living conditions, or sordid goings-on in Iowa? If there were, depictions of them don't show up on postcards, nor do images of unproductive farms, impoverished farm families, unemployed workers, children in sweatshops, dangerous factory working conditions—and this in spite of the fact that the agitations of the Populists were not very far in the past and the crusading and muckraking of the Progressive reformers were then going full blast. Those making their own postcards recorded only what was appealing and of value to them, while commercial photographers were guided by the dictates of their customers or by estimates of what would sell in the postcard racks. Positive, sunny, and high-toned images were likely to result in these circumstances.

But if the postcards ignore certain realities in favor of dwelling almost exclusively on what William Dean Howells called the "smiling aspects" of American life, they nonetheless do capture an authentic look of much of Iowa in the early twentieth century. Inasmuch as the images found on these cards had to pass muster with the many Iowans who made, bought, or mailed them, the composite picture they limn might be thought of as a kind of quasi-official or "authorized" collective portrait of the Hawkeye State. Even from this portrait, sans warts, much truth still escapes about the physical and mental worlds of the many Iowans who sat for it. What is portrayed jibes neatly, moreover, with what historians have concluded about American life and culture during the years covered by the postcards.

Finding these few years to be distinctive ones in the American saga, historians have had no difficulty reaching agreement about what set them apart, especially from the years that followed. In the words of Walter Lord, for instance, these were the Good Years—he suggests they might also be called the Confident Years, the Buoyant Years, the Spirited Years, even the Gold Years—"because whatever the trouble, people were sure they could fix it." Another historian, Richard Hofstadter, identifies the era's highly palpable sense of confidence and optimism as a "mood of hope," which gave to these years "an innocence and relaxation that cannot again be known." Echoing the foregoing themes, a third scholar, Henry F. May, also notes that these were years of "an almost intolerable placidity and complacency" linked to a stable "sense of what life means"—a sense which nonetheless crumbled fast with the coming of world war and the "end of American innocence." Finally, Frederick Lewis Allen, agreeing that this was a "time of complacency," observes that "each region, each town, each farm was far more dependent upon its own resources—its own produce, social events, amusements—than in later years"; as a result, underlying the era's advanced state of self-contentment can be discovered a profound insularity of life, mind, and culture, a condition soon to be made the target of satire and denunciation by Sinclair Lewis, H. L. Mencken, and other writers in the 1920s.

The photographic postcards shown here (as well as the much larger pool from which they were selected) richly support the aptness of these historians' conclusions. Leaping out of the cards is evidence of a people caught up in a parochial mentality, participating wholeheartedly in an exceedingly provincial culture, and organized into hundreds of vibrant but inward-looking and relatively self-contained communities populated by denizens of small towns and adjoining farms. Although social class lines actually were more glaring and rigidly observed in those years than now, evidence of them is muted in the postcards, which instead reflect a rather narrow range of gradations within one large, amorphous middle class. Scenes neither of poverty and deprivation nor of luxury and opulence but rather of solid, widespread middle-class comfort abound in these cards. Unquestionably, the people depicted therein seem to find a great satisfaction and joy in their lives, and we may be particularly apt to envy their capacity for feeling so much at ease in Zion.

But this same visual record throws off more than a few hints, too, of an innocence astoundingly oblivious to the world's realities and also teetering on the edge of smugness. In fact, what seems to radiate from the visages of some of the people depicted is not only an untroubled confidence that the good life they enjoy is theirs rightfully, perhaps simply by virtue of being Americans, but also a too easy conviction that "God's in His heaven, all's right with the world." Ponder, for instance, all that is communicated in the postcard on page 11 depicting an unidentified family from Stratford, Iowa. Decked out in their Sunday finest and perched in their new automobile (males in front, females to the rear, in accord with divine and natural law), the members of this family certainly betray in their faces no doubts about the essential rightness of things or about their entitlement to their newly achieved level of bourgeois comfort. When major challenges to American orthodoxy began to occur soon after this photograph was made, the jolt to persons possessing such serenity and certainty as expressed here must have been considerable.

Certainly most of what is depicted in these postcards seems quaint, old-fashioned, and distinct from our world today. But even in this Iowa of long ago, some developments of modernizing change and increasing linkage to national currents of culture were already afoot or even on the verge of dramatically altering life, and the postcards capture evidence of these, too—for example, the construction of new water and sewer systems in numerous small towns, the harnessing of steam power to an already far advanced mechanization of agriculture, the addition of streetcars and interurbans to the abundant intercity trains already serving many Iowa cities and towns, the widespread incidence of telephone and electric power lines, and perhaps above all the growing appearance nearly everywhere of automobiles, even though they were still a long way from supplanting horses. Another major nationalizing development leaving its traces on postcards (and, incidentally, also helping greatly to sustain the postcard craze of the early twentieth century) was the U.S. Post Office's new Rural Free Delivery (R.F.D.) system. By 1906, R.F.D. brought daily mail service to virtually every address in America, no matter how remote, and thus worked powerfully to diminish Iowa's cultural and physical isolation.

Because not everything found in photographic postcards can be covered in one book, postcards having a strong human interest have been given priority here. Depictions of public buildings, such as courthouses, libraries, banks, and churches—one of the largest categories of photographic postcards, usually well represented in books of this sort—have therefore been shortchanged in preference for postcards casting a more direct light on the lives and minds of the state's citizens. Depicting Iowans on farms and in towns, at home and in public, both at work and at play, these cards have then been grouped under chapter headings intended to highlight some of the characteristics of down-home mentality and culture discussed earlier. As a kind of poignant epilogue, a brief last chapter provides a few postcards showing Iowans during World War I, the calamitous event which, more immediately and visibly than any other, brought to a close the era depicted in these postcards.

The self-portrait of Iowa presented so beguilingly in the early photographic postcards is likely to call forth varying responses from readers. Some, for instance, may think they can discern a picture of a timeless, "essential" Iowa, one not gone but still in place and evident today. In fact, this view may have many fans; consider the state's hearty reception for a recent movie which showed contemporary Iowa looking much like the place depicted in these postcards and which also spawned a remarkable new booster slogan much in keeping with this view—"Is this Heaven? No, this is Iowa!" On the other hand, those who pine for the "good old days" probably would not only insist on reframing this question to read "*Was* this Heaven?" but also see in these postcards a vision of a long-departed idyllic Iowa. No matter how varied their perspectives may be, however, all readers ought to be able to find much direct enjoyment in poring over the splendid images reproduced here—images which may be variously charming, amusing, touching, or intriguing but are always packed with human interest and often have considerable aesthetic appeal as well. Few readers are likely to disagree, too, that having so many of these delightful and engaging postcard images is a boon putting us greatly in the debt of those many obscure but gifted photographers who helped to make the early decades of the twentieth century the "golden age" of postcards.

Many photographic studios,
such as this one in Oskaloosa,
specialized in putting customers'
images on postcards "while you
wait," often in novelty poses.

Professional photographers also left the studio to take the pictures wanted on postcards by customers. A peripatetic photographer is himself the subject of this postcard.

All Aboard for Clayton County Fair
NATIONAL, IOWA, SEPT. 8-9-10-11, 1908
H. LUEHSEN, SECY.

B-3

I don't care much for travel away across the sea,
A ride astride the old gray mare is good enough for me.

This charming
postcard advertising
the Clayton County Fair
also bears evidence of
a parochial outlook.

*A family from Stratford poses
for a postcard photograph which
captures an image redolent of
both material well-being and
self-satisfaction.*

The Rural Free Delivery system, which was of enormous benefit to Iowa's large rural population, was commemorated in many postcard images similar to this one from Richland.

1 : Hawkeyes

The fixing of likenesses of ordinary Iowans on custom-made photographic postcards was once sure to be an important part of the business of any commercial photographer in the state. Those working such venues as amusement parks, county fairs, and lakeside boardwalks lay in wait for Hawkeyes out on a lark, hoping to snare them with the prospect of being photographed wearing a barrel, flying high over the fair in a balloon, or doing some other outlandish thing bound to extract guffaws from friends and relatives receiving the postcards. More conventional portraits graced a much larger share of made-to-order postcards, however, and these generally carried the telltale marks of the small-town photographic studio and its accoutrements—such things as florid backdrops, tasseled drapes, Grecian columns and pedestals, paper moons, and other hackneyed props. Studio photographers, as well as free-lancing itinerants, were also available to take less formal, more personalized pictures on location at customers' homes or elsewhere. But this segment of postcard production they had to share with virtually anyone capable of snapping a shutter, once technological advances made postcard production easy, inexpensive, and therefore open to all.

Together, professionals and amateurs captured on postcards much individualized, homey, and often hokey fare featuring residents of the Hawkeye State. Many of these postcards were occasioned by events having personal significance in the lives of their subjects—for example, the arrival of a new baby, the passage of another year of life, a trip to Des Moines, a family picnic, graduation from high school, the purchase of a new automobile, or even nothing more momentous than a small gathering of good friends or the bagging of half a dozen pheasants on a hunting expedition. A special merit of these postcards, amply borne out by the examples in this chapter, is their depiction of run-of-the mill Iowans in some of the intimate relations of their lives. Here we see them, for instance, in connection with friends and family, hobbies and avocations, and such treasured possessions as house, automobile, shotgun, and dog.

We see them, that is, if they were Iowans of European ancestry. Images on vintage postcards of Iowans of other extractions range from uncommon to rare, obviously reflecting a major demographic reality of those early decades of this century: less than 1 percent—about 15,000 persons—of Iowa's population fell under the census denomination of "colored." Although Native Americans living on the Meskwaki settlement in Tama County were only a tiny portion of this category (about 350 persons), interesting postcard views of individuals and small groups of Meskwakis at Tama can still be found (one is presented here), thanks to the fact that they were produced in sufficient numbers to be sold as souvenirs to the settlement's visitors. And in spite of the even greater scarcity of Asian Americans living in Iowa, this chapter's selection of postcards includes one of a Chinese businessman in Sioux Rapids. However, photographic post-cards depicting African Americans—even though they were the largest component of Iowa's minority population—are among the most elusive of all today. None was lo-cated for use in this chapter, but several scenes at Buxton, a predominantly black min-ing community, now extinct, can be found in chapters three and four.

The elapse of more than three-quarters of a century has caused much in these highly personalized postcards to become intriguing or even downright mystifying to-day. Sometimes we will find ourselves asking about a particular postcard image: Who are these people? Why are they posed as they are? What are they doing and why are they doing it? Why was this image ever put on a postcard? Moreover, some of the whimsical content of the postcards will not elicit today the responses that could be counted on more than seventy-five years ago, and sometimes, too, we may spot humor where none was intended. But these are minor and inevitable vicissitudes of the pas-sage of time, and, far from diminishing the enjoyment to be found in these postcards, they seem often to enhance the human interest, good humor, and charm distilled in so many of them. Certainly these are qualities in plentiful supply in the small gallery of Hawkeyes presented here.

The author's grandfather and aunt, vaudeville performers from Atlantic.

Hat and dog are distinctive touches in this portrait of a woman in New Sharon.

"Mr. Stryka" and his accordion, somewhere in Iowa.

*Twin sisters in
Oxford Junction.*

A big Ames attraction.

A Muscatine
photographer gives
a novel twist to a familiar
studio prop, the
paper moon.

Three callow Iowa youths "flying high" over Sioux City.

*A message from an
Iowa belle on vacation in
Colorado: "Dear Katie: I am
the wild cowboy from the plains
of Colo. I start for the ranch next
week. This is our cabin and
horse as you see. Hurrah
for the wild west and
fine health. Yours,
Bertha."*

A. J. PHILLIPS
POCAHONTAS, IOWA

Drum Major Iowa Department
National Association of Civil War Musicians.

A Pocahontas man drums up attention for himself and an unusual Civil War veterans group.

Mrs. C. F. Hillstrom's home Pomeroy, Ia

Many Iowans, such
as Mrs. C. F. Hillstrom
of Pomeroy, posed proudly
with their houses for
photographic postcards.

A big game hunter from Bellevue demonstrates the need for stricter hunting laws.

*C. Fong and his laundry
in Sioux Rapids. "This is the
fellow that gave and cooked
our duck for Xmas dinner."*

*Two scrawny plants
potted in tin cans add a
bizarre touch to this studio
shot in Oskaloosa.*

A Des Moines dandy
and his dog.

*From Marengo, an
intriguing interior shot:
why was it taken and why
was it then put on
a postcard?*

*All three members
of this Iowa family leave
unusual images for us
to ponder today.*

*An Iowa family at the
Meskwaki settlement
in Tama.*

THE NORTON TRIPLETS

Three sons of George and Bertha Norton, of Osceola, Iowa, born February 19, 1910 :: :: ::

EDWIN   HAROLD   DONALD

Big news from Osceola.

*Father and daughter?
Grandfather and
granddaughter? In
any event, a striking
photograph from
Oxford Junction.*

*A child on Christmas
Day, 1908, in Algona. Note
the Christmas tree on the table
and other details caught
in this parlor scene.*

A photographer in Washington produced this charming picture of a charming subject.

AT 5 YRS. AT 13 YRS. AT 14 YRS. AT THE PRESENT. 17 YRS. 5 MO.

"BILLY WINTER."

At the august age of
seventeen years, five months,
Billy Winter of New Sharon takes
us on a review of images from
earlier stages in his life.

Murray   Howard   Florence

Children of a politician from Wapello. "Three reasons why I want to be County Recorder, and anything you can do June 3 to assist me will be greatly appreciated. Yours truly, Homer H. Winder."

Three "hunters" from Reinbeck.

*"1st, 2nd, & 3rd grades.
These are the worst convicts
we have. I.S.P. [Iowa State
Penitentiary, Fort Madison],
Hans."*

This card was produced in Marshalltown. Who are these people? What's going on? Note the revolver in the girl's left hand.

Shelby, Iowa, Aug. 24th 1906. We were having a good time. Anna.

Young women "having a good time" in Shelby.

*Young women having
a better time drinking beer
in Oxford Junction.*

In an Osceola photographer's studio, two fun-loving Iowa lads pose with bottles of foul-looking booze in hand.

In a more innocent age, a hemp plant provides a setting for a game of peek-a-boo in Colo.

2 : The Kind We Raise

SOME IOWA PRODUCTS. *"Bringing in the Sheaves."*

The history of any of the American states should "begin with the land itself"—so claims Joseph F. Wall in *Iowa: A Bicentennial History*. In the case of Iowa, however, Wall contends that "the land serves as more than an introduction. It is the major story line." Among the impressive facts about Iowa's land which he brings forward are these: an astonishing 98 percent of Iowa's land is under cultivation, a percentage larger than that of any other state; more than 70 percent of Iowa's land is rated Grade A—that is, of premium quality; and one out of every four acres of Grade A land in the United States lies within Iowa's borders. Wall's conclusion—"agriculture has always been the omniculture of Iowa"—may exaggerate the dominance of Iowa's agriculture and the determinative force of the state's rich land, but certainly he is right to argue that Iowa was destined to be an agricultural state of the front rank and that that destiny has had a profound effect on the substance and flavor of life in the state.

By the opening years of the twentieth century, Iowa was already well known for its bountiful agriculture and could make a strong claim to be the quintessential farm state. Much evidence from the popular culture of that era suggests, too, that when Americans envisioned the typical Iowan, what came to mind was the hayseed, the country bumpkin, the hick from the farm. In truth, however, at the start of the century, only 40 percent of employed Iowans over the age of ten were engaged in agricultural pursuits. This percentage had already fallen considerably from its 1880 level, and it has continued its downward path ever since. Far from indicating a long-run decline in the importance of agriculture in Iowa, this trend actually registers the ever-expanding pro-ductivity of Iowa's farms and farmers—an astonishing performance surely indicating capabilities beyond those of mere hayseeds or bumpkins.

Clearly entitled to take great pride in being champion producers of food, Iowa's farmers well into this century doubtless also incorporated in their self-image some fa-miliar notions, traceable to Thomas Jefferson, about farmers being the "chosen people of God" and the foundation of a good social and political order. Indeed, many other Iowans might have joined with the farmers in believing that Iowa faithfully embodied Jeffersonian ideals. Several of the state's most prominent features appeared to give sup-port to this belief—for instance, the absence in Iowa of the large metropolitan centers that Jefferson so dreaded (this absence, Wall notes, is a major consequence of the rich-ness of Iowa's land). Consider, too, the pronounced Jeffersonian flavor of these facts: in 1905, Iowa's farm land was comprised of an enormous number of farms of modest size—209,000 farms, averaging 160 acres each—a full two-thirds of which were owned by the persons who farmed them and lived on them. Here, it might have seemed, was a substantial realization of the economic foundation which Jefferson claimed was needed to sustain a republic of virtuous, independent, and equal citizens.

In one very major way, however, Iowa's farmers diminished their claim to wear the mantle of Jefferson: from the start they were not his beloved "yeomen" (that is, subsistence farmers) but rather commercial farmers, specializing in the production of various cash crops or livestock for sale in distant markets. From the Jeffersonian point of view, this was a grave misstep, sure to undercut the independence of farmers by making them dependent on market fluctuations and also entangling them with powerful, inimical interests (at first, bankers, to which later were added various monopolists, especially those who operated railroads and grain elevators). When Iowa's farmers, and the nation's farmers generally, turned to commercial farming, they became, in effect, business speculators, a fact which William Jennings Bryan acknowledged in 1896 in his "Cross of Gold" speech but which would have dismayed Jefferson.

It was farming-conducted-as-a-business, however, that enabled Iowa's choice farm land to be put to maximum productive use, brought forth the immense corn production on which Iowa's fame as the Tall Corn State is based, and eventually led to the state's additional eminence as a leading pork and soybean producer. True enough, in the 1920s and 1930s Iowa farmers learned that there was some point to Jefferson's warnings about the vagaries of markets. In the earliest years of this century, however, farmers in Iowa were receiving good prices for their products—in fact, the favorable ratio of these prices from 1910 to 1914 compared to the prices farmers had to pay for goods used in production was later taken as the measure of full parity in federal farm price support programs. If further evidence is needed of the relative prosperity of Iowa farmers during these years, one need only note, too, that their fidelity to the Republican party stood firm throughout; indeed, on three occasions Iowa's voters resoundingly had rejected the presidential bids of Bryan, purportedly the farmers' champion. Apparently, most of Iowa's farmers did not believe that the embattled, hard-pressed, and ill-used farmers for whom the Great Commoner claimed to speak included them.

Photographic postcards can be found today covering virtually every type of agriculture in Iowa in the early decades of this century and virtually every phase of farming, too—plowing, planting, harvesting, threshing, shelling, and many other kinds of farm activities, such as barn building, well digging, and wood splitting. In depicting a time which was a relatively good one for farmers, the postcards convey strong suggestions of prosperity, tranquillity, and happiness down on the farm. Underlying and sustaining these values was Iowa's celebrated agricultural productivity, which also gets much play in these early postcards. Images of promotional displays of Iowa as the "Land of Plenty" and boastful tall-tale concoctions showing gigantic hogs or enormous ears of corn (often labeled with some variant of "The Kind We Raise in Iowa") proclaimed Iowa's farming prowess, but so did a myriad of realistic images—for example, those depicting prizewinning hogs or corn, wagons loaded with grain lined up for delivery at elevators, or the steam-powered machines and other advanced equipment which helped so greatly to keep Iowa at the forefront of farm states. The postcard images reproduced in this chapter are representative of the great mass of early photographic postcards which helped bring Iowa to the world's attention as the premier farm state.

This selection also discloses another characteristic of these postcards: they often have aesthetic appeal as well as documentary value. On occasion, early photographers brought forth striking and beautiful results. Perhaps these humble artisans did better work then they knew. Or perhaps they simply recognized and took advantage of a fact well known to every Iowan: there is much to gratify the eye in the rural landscape of Iowa.

IOWA'S EXHIBIT—HORN OF PLENTY.
AGRICULTURAL BUILDING.
STATE FAIR GROUNDS.
DES MOINES, IOWA.

Iowa as a cornucopia spewing corn—also used as the state's exhibit at the Panama-Pacific Exposition in San Francisco in 1915.

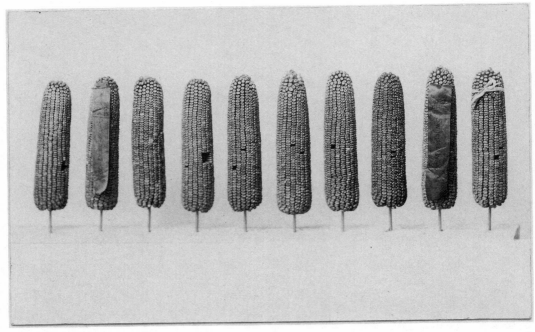

*"Shenandoah, Ia., Dec. 3rd,
1911. Elizabeth: This card illustrates
the ten ears of corn with which I
won the Sweepstakes Thropy* [sic]
*at Farmer's Institute last year. The
ear farthest to the right is the one
with which I won $10.00 at the
State Fair. Fred."*

110 acres at $ 255

Near Clarksville. The inscription suggests that the couple in the buggy may just have bought this farm, which in appearance and size was characteristic of a great many Iowa farms early in this century.

If the foreground of this picture of "good plowing" near Cherokee is too dark for easy viewing, much of the blame lies with the black richness of Iowa's topsoil.

Iowa Corn, Essex, Ia

An enterprising photographer in Essex concocted this wonderful variation on a familiar theme.

THE KIND OF CORN WE RAISE AT HUXLEY, IA.   660.

*A Boone photographer
skillfully inserted this giant ear
of corn into a photograph of a
commercial street in Huxley.*

The same photographer
put the same ear of corn to
work on the Main Streets of
Springville and other Iowa
towns.

One of the best tall-tale postcards saluting Iowa's hog-raising prowess.

A prizewinning hog from Ralston appears to be not much smaller than its tall-tale counterpart.

Two proud hog farmers
show off the ribbons which the
champ (standing between them)
has just won at the North Iowa
Fair in Mason City.

A groom displays some residents of the farm of J. C. Ritchie, a leading horse-breeder in the state, in Stratford.

"*Everybody
Milks in
Iowa*"

*Don't miss the
cows and the folks
and the fun—and
the milking—at the
Iowa State Dairy
Convention and
Dairy Cattle
Congress, Water-
loo, Iowa, October
13th to 18th.*

*Promoters of an
annual conclave of dairy
farmers in Waterloo slipped
into hyperbolic mode with
a claim that "Everybody
Milks in Iowa."*

EVERYBODY MILKS IN IOWA

(An Ode to the Cow Dedicated to the Dairy Industry)
Tune: Everybody Works But Father

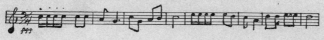

Everybody milks in Iowa,
  We all like the cow.
Pinning our faith to bessy,
  Has made our neighbors bow.
Everybody milks in Iowa,
  Even Sister Rae,
Everybody does the milking
  In   I   O   A.

Everybody milks in Iowa,
  Summer and winter time,
Makes no difference to Iowa,
  They milk rain or shine.
Soil is growing richer,
  Debts all cleared away,
Just because they're milking
  In   I   O   A.

Everybody milks in Iowa,
  Let me tell you that,
Buying auto-mobiles
  With the butter-fat;
If the grain crops fail them,
  They don't move away,
Just keep right on milking
  In   I   O   A.

Everybody milks in Iowa,
  Hear me, what I say,
Live on milk and honey
  While the cows eat hay,
Mother's quit her washing,
  So has Sister Ann,
Everybody's gone to milking,
  Even my old man.
                —E. T. Sadler.

**Come to Water-
loo and Help
Us Sing**

*At the Iowa State
Dairy Convention
and Dairy Cattle
Congress, Water-
loo, Iowa, Octo-
ber 9th to 14th*

*"Everybody Milks in
Iowa" was also the title of
a song, whose four stanzas
were loosed on the world in
this advertisement for the
big Waterloo event in
1911.*

An advertisement for two of the many fairs in Iowa boosting livestock breeding.

"This cow bought this automobile for this dairy farmer in six years. The cow, the automobile, the farmer, his family and herd of cows will all be at the big dairy show in Waterloo, Oct. 10 to 15th [1910]. Merchants will refund railroad fares. Come."

Creamery Day at Fern, Ia.

*Was creamery day at Fern
also an occasion for a spirited
rendition of "Everybody Milks
in Iowa"?*

*"Mrs. Willie Weinberg and
her turkeys on their farm near
Plainfield."*

Shipping apples in Glenwood.
Apple growing was a considerable
part of Iowa's agriculture; by 1910
the state placed sixth among all of
the states in apple production.

"The start for R. Jenson's barn." Farmer Jenson didn't let faulty camera work stand in the way of producing this postcard record of the big event.

*Farmers gather for an auction
at a farm near Sandyville.*

Although by the early 1900s farming was highly mechanized in Iowa, horses still were often used to pull the machines.

*As steam increasingly
replaced horses as a source
of power, Iowa's much vaunted
agricultural productivity
steadily advanced.*

The advantages of steam-powered equipment are illustrated in this scene of the laying up of hay.

*Iowa as the "land of
plenty" was celebrated
in many photographic postcards
bearing appealing scenes of
farmers delivering grain to
elevators, such as this one
from Walcott.*

ELEVATORS AND MILLS
PAULLINA IA

*The elevators and mills
of Paullina comprised a scene
of striking beauty in the hands
of a gifted postcard
photographer.*

*Buildings in Iowa
farmyards often had the
makings of attractive postcard
scenes, as in this photograph
of a farm near Jefferson.*

*A town-dweller could easily
be fetched by the bucolic charms
of the Iowa countryside and the
pleasure of communing with
cows lazing in the fields.*

Iowa's attractive rural landscape was caught in this scene near Marion featuring a wooden bridge.

3 : Everything's Up to Date in River City

Although Iowa is usually thought of in terms of its many farms, it has always been a state of small towns as well. As Iowa's land was rapidly occupied and put under tillage in the mid-nineteenth century, towns appeared every ten miles or so to provide goods and services needed by farmers and also markets (or access to markets) for their crops. By no means did all of these towns prosper; one major factor affecting the fate of a town in the second half of that century was the town's proximity to rail service. Thanks both to Iowa's strategic location and to the high value of its farm products, however, an extensive rail network reaching every part of the state developed quickly. As early as 1880, Iowa had 5,235 miles of railroad tracks, an amount placing it high among all of the states and insuring that many small towns would stay alive into the next century. In 1905 there were nearly 800 incorporated towns in the state.

In spite of the large number of Iowa towns, throughout the nineteenth century town residents were far outnumbered by rural residents; in 1890, fewer than two of every five Iowans lived in incorporated municipalities. That proportion was on the rise, however, and by 1905 town-dwellers came very close to equalling half of Iowa's population. (Today they make up more than 75 percent.)

According to the 1905 *Census of Iowa*, most of the growth in Iowa's urban population occurred in the "larger cities" of the state, by which were meant "towns of 25,000 or over." There were only seven in this category, however, of which three barely made it over the threshold figure, three others hovered around 40,000, and the largest—Des Moines—had a mere 75,000 residents. In other words, Iowa's growing "larger cities" in 1905 were, in truth, what historian Joseph Wall concludes they have remained ever since—"small towns grown somewhat large."

Because Iowa's many towns were objects of great pride to their residents, photographers had before them a lucrative market for postcard images of the "old home town." Photographic postcards recorded many features of hundreds of Iowa communities ranging in size from the so-called larger cities to tiny hamlets and country crossroad villages. This chapter focuses on postcard images of the landscape and other physical aspects of those communities, leaving to later chapters a look at postcards depicting various aspects of life in Iowa's towns.

A leading student of American small towns, John Jakle, has observed that "postcard photographers sought the unique in small-town landscapes, but tended to find the typical instead." Certainly this is borne out by their large output of images of such recurring landscape features as courthouses, churches, public libraries, post offices, train depots, city parks, tree-lined residential streets, town squares, and—most important of all—Main Street.

In the nineteenth century, lithographers seeking to fill the demand for prints of America's cities and towns had also "sought the unique" but "found the typical" in their customary renderings of whole cities or towns by means of the bird's-eye view. Usually the bird's-eye view was not a possibility for postcard photographers, however, and the view that was instead used most often to represent a community in its entirety was that of its commercial Main Street or, in towns having a town square, views of the business streets bounding the square. Far from deciding this convention on their own, postcard photographers were simply acting in conformance with a widespread American belief that Main Street was a town's most important street, the fixed point in relation to which all else in town could be located and oriented, the place most expressive of the forward-looking and go-getting spirit of a town. However, the many postcards depicting small-town Main Streets must at least have helped fix stereotypical images of Main Street in the minds of Iowans and Americans generally. Possibly they also reinforced Main Street's standing as one of the major symbols in terms of which Americans have thought (whether positively or negatively) about small towns and small-town life.

In the quest for greater comforts and conveniences as well as for an enhanced base for the local economy, the residents of Iowa's towns in the earliest decades of this century avidly pursued civic improvements—in smaller towns, such basics as water, sewer, electric, and telephone service, and, in larger towns, such amenities as street cars and paved sidewalks and streets. Evidence of civic improvements can often be spotted in postcards—for instance, the overhead maze of electric, telephone, and trolley wires appearing in some of the scenes of business districts reproduced in this book. In fact, many postcards were made for the express purpose of documenting the latest developments in town, such as the laying of sewer tiles, the paving of sidewalks, or the acquisition of a new device for cleaning the streets. Two subjects appearing very often in photographic postcards were the town's new water tower and its fire-fighting equipment.

From today's perspective, sewer pipes and water towers may seem ludicrous subjects for postcards. At the start of the present century, however, such mundane urban features, and many services which we take for granted, were far from universal, and their arrival in town marked a real advance. Postcards not only commemorated these major strides forward but also expressed an understandable local pride. People receiving these postcards in the mail would be informed, too, that the sender lived in an up-to-date, "live wire" town on the move. Imparting this message was a major concern of town boosters in that era—a concern, incidentally, often satirized by a type of tall-tale postcard (several examples are included in this chapter) in which big-city features, such as street cars and elevated trains, were superimposed on photographs of the Main Streets of very small towns.

Although towns did not have to have many thousands of residents to have street cars, the basic mode of transportation in and around Iowa's towns in those years remained the horse-drawn vehicle. Nonetheless, automobiles had already begun to make a strong showing; there were only 799 of them in Iowa in 1905, but by 1915 the number had soared to 147,078. In not many more years, of course, the private automobile would not only completely supplant the horse and then the street car as modes of intracity transportation but would also have unanticipated consequences profoundly affecting Iowa's small towns. The early photographic postcards, however, throw off no hints of the revolutionary role that automobiles would soon play. In many downtown scenes (especially those in very small towns), horse-drawn vehicles outnumber automobiles or the latter don't appear at all, and the large clusterings of automobiles depicted on some postcards are more likely to be the result of a rally, a race, or some other special event than a foretaste of future traffic jams.

An abundance of photographic postcards depicting trains and depots indicates that trains were the dominant mode of travel between cities, a position they would hold for many more years. At the same time, at least some Iowans had begun to dream of a future in which the private automobile would be an alternative means of intercity travel. However, a formidable obstacle lying in the way was Iowa's roads, which were notoriously unfit for automobile use in wet weather. Several postcards reproduced here capture the reality of the state's bad roads, reflect the rising concern to "get Iowa out of the mud," and provide evidence of the arrival of a new major problem—highway accidents and automobile wrecks.

A common Saturday in Berlin, Iowa

The shadow at lower left suggests that this bird's-eye view of "a common Saturday" was probably taken atop a grain elevator in Berlin (whose name was changed to Lincoln during World War I).

*A clever way to show
off one of Boone's attractive
brick-paved commercial
streets.*

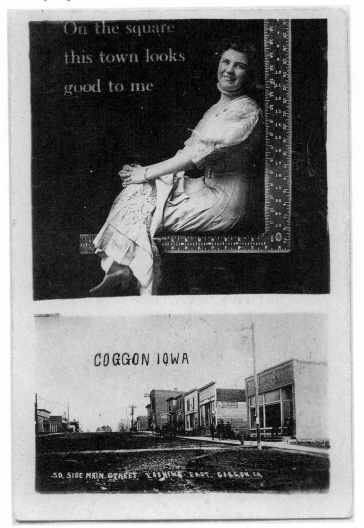

To make this gag
work, the photographer
had to give more space to
the woman sitting on the
square than to Coggon's
Main Street.

*A child walks in complete
safety across Main Street to
the Blue Front Hotel in
downtown Rubio.*

Main Street was a residential
street in Buxton, a predominantly
African American coal-mining
town in which most of the
commercial life centered
on a company store.

*Lots of buggies but
no automobiles grace
this unpaved commercial
street in Sidney.*

SECOND ST EAST TRAER IA - 13

Like the main commercial streets of many other Iowa towns, this one in Traer was wide enough to accommodate both automobiles and horse-drawn vehicles.

The large number of automobiles in downtown Slater probably had something to do with a Labor Day celebration.

*A trolley car makes its
way down a very crowded
Main Street in Mason City.*

*As trolleys crossed the
Bremer Avenue Bridge in
Waverly, passengers could
read an advertisement for
a marvelous elixir that
"relieves fatigue."*

Walnut Street, looking East, Des Moines, Iowa.

A commercial street in Des Moines had more of a "big city" look than did most other commercial streets in Iowa.

The inviting Hotel Elmira
awaited the weary drummer or
any other traveler whom chance
might bring to Elmira.

In 1910 Rowley's Restaurant in Ward was beginning to cater to the horseless carriage trade.

In superimposing the streetcar so expertly, the photographer created a convincing scene of bustle and progress in Dawson.

7122. ELEVATED ALTON. IOWA. IN YEAR 1925

In this depiction of Alton in the not-too-distant future, the photographer cleverly satirized the hype and big aspirations of small-town boosters.

Perhaps word of the germ theory of disease had not yet reached What Cheer when this postcard depicting a town pump and communal drinking cup was made.

Postcard views of new water towers often showed the construction workers posing on top or sides of the tank, as in this example from New Hampton.

PUTTING IN
WATER MAINS
ADAIR. IA.

1911. DINSMORE
PHOTO

Indoor plumbing
lay just ahead for the
residents of Adair.

This postcard depicting telephone operators indicated that Akron had telephone service, a stride forward of which any small town could be proud.

"MODERN SANITATION" AT WORK IN SHENANDOAH IOWA

First, hard-surfaced streets, then the latest technology for cleaning those streets—clearly Shenandoah was a city on the move.

Iowa City Fire Department, Iowa City, Iowa.

*Two benchmarks of
urban progress are registered
in this postcard from Iowa City—
a professional fire department
and a Carnegie library (the
large stone building on
the right).*

"This is Gary's buss and Ray is in the buss." Modern bus service was available in Prescott.

*The train depot at Fonda
is shown here as an example
of the hundreds of images of
depots that ended up on
postcards.*

Citizens Meet Construction Train
Southeast Town Limits
Quasqueton, Sept. 2, 1912.

Train service began in
Quasqueton three days after
the town's citizens and brass
band turned out to welcome the
construction crew and watch
them complete the job.

Any motorist braving Iowa's notoriously bad roads was soon certain to be mired in mud, like this motorist near Wellman.

*This float in a parade in
Iowa City in 1913 spoke for
all motorists in Iowa.*

*A Mason City cement
company heralds the first
cement-paved, intercity Iowa
highway, begun in 1913
and completed in 1917.*

This Sioux City hotel was
the end point of an automobile
tour promoting development of
a "Hawkeye Highway Shortcut"
from Storm Lake to Sioux City
via Kingsley.

State Center, Iowa.
Aug. 16th 1910.
Bottom side up, Engine still
running. Nobody hurt.
Yours truly,
J. A. Mingers

Although deaths in automobile wrecks had already begun to occur in Iowa, these motorists from State Center seem remarkably nonchalant about this accident.

*Three young motorists from
Oelwein find their auto accident
to be good subject matter for
postcard mementos to send
to friends.*

4 : How We Do Things

We will appreciate your Holiday Trade
E. S. Lambert.

At the outset of this century, much more of the commercial life of
Iowa was carried on in small towns and by small businesses than
is true in our time. Today's small towns are often only pale copies
of the thriving communities and important commercial hubs
they once were, casualties of the major economic changes oc-
curring in this century. Even towns still appearing to prosper
have likely undergone a stressful shifting of much of their commercial activities from downtown business districts to strips and
malls nearer the edges of town.

When small towns really hummed, however, virtually all of their economic activities were concentrated in the heart of town. In larger towns, this consisted of several contiguous business blocks and, in smaller towns, Main Street or the streets enclosing the town square. There, small retail stores and shops—as well as banks, restaurants, and the offices of lawyers, doctors, and dentists—catered to the needs and at least some of the wants of residents of the town and of the nearby farms. And businesses not situated there—perhaps a blacksmith shop, livery stable, or lumber and coal yard—were not likely to be very far away.

In those palmier days of downtown business districts, any up-and-coming Iowa town had at least one organization of merchants devoted to promoting the merits of the town and its businesses. In Des Moines, local boosters proclaimed Iowa's capital to be "The City That Does Things," even spelling out a variant of this self-proclaimed accolade with flowers on a lawn in a city park. "Doing things" was already a familiar term of babbittry, however, and was also available for use by any town or state in a kind of tall-tale postcard bearing the inscription "How We Do Things in ———." It is unlikely that other cities and towns in Iowa would have conceded to Des Moines exclusive rights to this title. In one way or another, all claimed an excellence in "doing things."

Photographic postcards depicting scenes of a town's Main Street or of "A Busy Day in ———," examples of which were presented in the previous chapter, helped to foster the impression of a prosperous town on the move and "doing things." But the ultimate concern of all town boosters was, of course, the prosperity of their individual businesses, and these they often sought to promote through the use of postcards. Interior or exterior views can be found today of virtually every kind of store or business operating on Main Street. Both types of views are represented in this chapter.

Although these postcards were intended for advertising uses, it is hard not to conclude that other purposes were involved, too. An interior view allowed a merchant not only to display the store's wares but also to strike a proud pose, perhaps to show off the size of the store's sales force or to be seen in the act of selling—that is, "doing things." An exterior view, which usually showed the merchant, the store's employees, and sometimes a few customers standing in front, provided a visual record of the store as it appeared within a larger social setting, often that of Main Street; it was the kind of picture which, blown up to larger size and framed, one might expect to find hanging (next to the framed "First Dollar Earned") in the proprietor's office, and perhaps sometimes it actually was put to this use. When either kind of view went into the mail, a merchant could give graphic expression to feelings of pride in entrepreneurial achievement as well as convey a sales message written on the reverse side of the postcard.

Businesses of the kinds found on the Main Streets of Iowa small towns were not the only ones depicted in photographic postcards. Images representative of many types of commercial and industrial firms operating in Iowa—ranging from coal mines and limestone quarries through plant nurseries, breweries, and factories making such things as buttons, automobiles, washing machines, and clay pots—ended up on postcards, a sample of which are reproduced here. Even more abundant were postcard images of Iowans at work at a very broad range of callings; workers depicted included carpenters, house painters, ditch diggers, road building crews, railroad workers, teachers, trolly conductors, newspaper editors, barbers, and bankers, to name just a few (in addition to the Main Street retailers noted above and the farm workers taken account of in an earlier chapter). So numerous and varied were these postcards that the few illustrations presented here cannot do justice to the genre.

Unlike those depicting individual Main Street stores, the many postcards which so richly and appealingly document the work activities of Iowans early in this century were not intended for advertising uses. Why, then, were they made? And what is the significance of their large number? Perhaps the many happy scenes of Iowans at work simply indicate that, in an economic sense, those really were good years. Or maybe they also express the ebullience, optimism, and confidence which historians claim characterized the mood of many Americans in those years. At the very least, these postcard images hint that a zeal for "doing things" may have been a widely shared impulse of that age and not merely the product of a self-serving creed promoted by small-town merchants.

GITY HALL PARK.

*In the zip department,
Des Moines boosters were
the equals of George F. Babbitt
and his go-getting pals in
Zenith.*

These five benefactors
offered one-stop shopping
in Webster City for dry goods,
shoes, hardware, sporting goods,
furniture, groceries, embalming,
and undertaking.

*These stores in Garwin,
including the one offering
both furniture and undertaking,
were characteristic of businesses
found on Main Streets
throughout Iowa.*

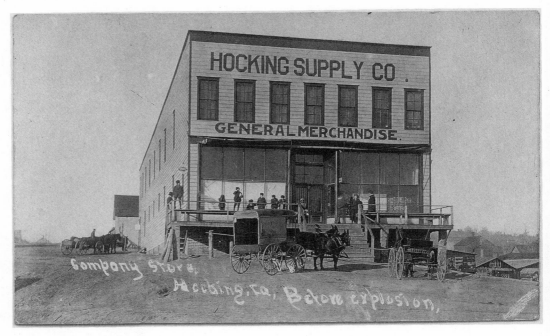

A company store located
in Iowa coal-mining country
in Hocking. The reference to
an explosion is a reminder of
one of the great hazards of
mining.

This combination restaurant and bakery in Casey appears to have no name other than "cafe." A sign on the theater next door advertises Saturday matinees.

*A crate of sardines
is among the items being
auctioned in this street sale
in downtown Goodell.*

*These men in Bradford
look ready to do things—
but what?*

This "auto livery" in Lenox
is a salesroom and perhaps also
a service garage for Buicks. Note
the boot used as a sign for the
business next door.

Taken May 20 – 1910

Clare.

Clare stands in the
doorway of a general
store in Sioux Rapids: "I
look like I felt alright," she
confided cryptically to
friend Daisy.

*"Dear Brother and
Sister, Kindly Rem[em]ber
me" seems an unlikely message
to accompany this image of
a grocer and store in
Bethlehem.*

Millinery Department. Leader Store. Gowrie.

*In the millinery department
of the Leader Store in Gowrie,
clerks and customers are almost
lost from sight amidst a jumble
of hats, flowers, vines, and
floral-print wallpaper.*

*A jeweler displays his
wares, which include sewing
machines, in a high-toned
shop in Waterloo.*

The Fair, Ida Grove, Iowa

Although china and
glasswares appear to be
the specialties of the Fair
Store in Ida Grove, on the
right are a few shelves of
books and a display rack
full of picture postcards.

A doctor's office in Des Moines? Note stirrups on the chair—and also the spittoon, jerry-rigged lighting system, and, on the door, a pin-up drawing on buckskin of an Indian woman.

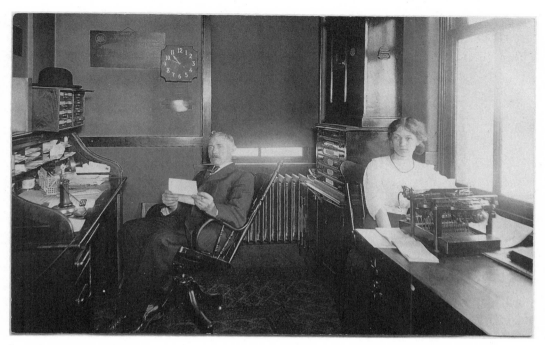

*Less perplexing than the
preceding image is this depiction
of a modern business office in
Des Moines.*

*Staff members enjoy a
moment of repose seized
from the hectic pace of getting
out the weekly* Tribune *in
Eddyville.*

"Doing things" in the dining hall of the state penitentiary in Fort Madison.

*This scene of a big
construction project under
way in Stanhope is representative
of a great many postcard views
showing work crews pausing
at their work for a
photograph.*

"Voluntiers" [sic] *pitch
in to help a financially pinched
friend in Haverhill put in a
cement sidewalk.*

Grave diggers prepare to bury horses in Herndon. Might the city slicker (sitting on horse at right) be a state or county health officer?

*Making ice the
old-fashioned way
in Victor.*

*Postcard scenes of
women doing domestic
chores are not common.
Here two sisters in
Osceola wash
clothes.*

*A kitchen scene in
Homestead, one of the
Amana colonies.*

In the early 1900s, oil was still delivered in Cedar Rapids by horse-drawn tank.

*At West Liberty, racks of
dressed chickens are taken
aboard a refrigerated
railroad car.*

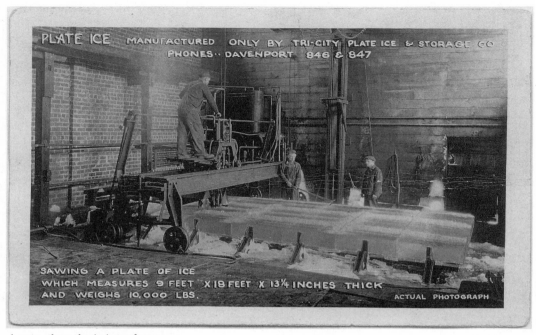

A very clear depiction of one phase of production at an ice factory in Davenport.

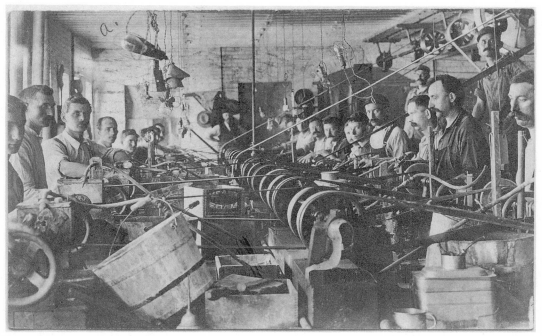

In a factory in Muscatine,
workers make buttons from
clam shells.

The placement of the two human figures in this photograph reveals the immense size of the kilns and factory of the What Cheer Clay Products Co.

*Three mineworkers pose
beside a coal vein in a mine
near Lucas.*

*Payday at the Buxton
coal mines.*

5 : Booster Days

In the judgment of small-town boosters, the greatest evil was "knocking"—that is, belonging to the "sour grapes crowd," questioning aspects of the small-town worldview, turning a cold shoulder to the backslapping camaraderie of local merchants, failing to extend a glad hand in support of their schemes and projects. The obligation of all responsible residents of a town, especially those who had businesses there, was to join in hyping the town's virtues, fostering town spirit, and constantly pushing the town's commercial well-being. "Boost, don't knock!" became the buzzwords of the day, as denizens of Main Streets everywhere pitched in to promote civic activities which mixed sales campaigns, hoopla, entertainment, and right-thinking.

The booster activity reaching the highest amperage and tapping the most ergs of citizens in any small town was an annual gala known, in generic terms, as booster days. Although this event was sometimes actually named Booster Days, often it was called Old Settler Days or the Merchants' Carnival, and perhaps oftener it carried a unique title distinguishing it from all other such events elsewhere—for example, $1,000 Day, Melon Days, Potato Days, and Sauerkraut Days, several of which are commemorated in postcards in this chapter. No matter what this major event was called, however, it usually had standard components: a street carnival, band concerts, perhaps a baseball game pitting a local nine against one from a rival town, and, invariably, a parade. This last item was often a major production, featuring bands, marching units from the local fraternal lodges and police and fire departments, and floats advertising local businesses, organizations, and sometimes even churches.

If their motivation for sponsoring booster days was, at bottom, a commercial one, the merchants nonetheless put on an entertaining show. Another occasion also eagerly awaited each year (and, for its planning and execution, probably drawing on many of the same persons and organizations producing booster days) was the Independence Day celebration. The impulse behind this event was patriotism rather than commerce, and the focus of boosting was the nation rather than the town. Still, the celebration of Independence Day (and of other patriotic holidays, such as Decoration Day) had much in common with the goings-on of booster days—band music, a parade, games, and pageantry, to cite the most obvious features. Surely these celebrations also had much the same significance for the citizens of Iowa's small towns—that is, they were an expression and an affirmation of the shared life of the town, but at the same time they provided a welcome break from the everyday drabness and tedium of that life.

The annual county fair played a similar role, as did the state fair. For the latter, the grandest of all booster events in Iowa, a surprisingly large number of families, from both farms and towns, made their way to Des Moines each year for the better part of a week—a fairly difficult and expensive expedition in the early decades of this century.

Although all of these events—booster days, Independence Day festivities, county and state fairs—live on, their character and also the importance of each in the lives of most Iowans today have been profoundly affected by the many demographic, economic, and social changes taking place in this century. Moreover, each of these events today must compete with an enormous range of cultural offerings and entertainment options available to Iowans, even those who live in the smallest village or on the remotest farm. Once, however, when the lives of most Iowans were largely circumscribed by the boundaries of the small towns in or near which they resided, the various expressions of boosting—parades, street carnivals, and fairs—provided an excitement that otherwise was in short supply. The great importance that these special occasions had in those earlier days is suggested by the many scenes of boosting activities captured on photographic postcards.

*The Keota Ladies Band
leads the town's Booster Day
parade.*

Three rows of automobiles
stretch to the vanishing point
in Dyersville's long parade
on $1,000 Day.

*One of the less flamboyant floats
entered in the Merchants Carnival
parade in Maquoketa.*

*The fire brigade prepares
to march in the same booster
parade in Maquoketa.*

Booster celebrations often joined themes of patriotism and commerce, as in the floats in this parade in Latimer.

FARMER'S PICNIC
WEST SIDE PARK
ROCHESTER IA
AUG 29, 08.

Old settlers' reunions and farmers' picnics, such as this one in Rochester, were variant forms of small-town booster celebrations.

*Commercial drummers
have their day in the limelight
in Cherokee. Do their raincoats
and umbrellas symbolize the
rigors of the traveling life?*

A float plugging Coffin's store (in background) is ready to join the parade on Melon Day, an annual event in Cone (a.k.a. Conesville) celebrating Muscatine County's best-known crop.

*Ackley's annual Sauer-Kraut
Day must have fallen on hard
times when World War I brought
anti-German sentiment and the
featured dish was renamed
"liberty cabbage."*

*An acrobatic act by the
"Upside Down Geraldas" in
Vail's street carnival bedazzles
a well-scrubbed small-town
crowd.*

At this street carnival in Lenox,
the most popular offering appears
to be a sideshow act featuring
"The Devil Fish Woman."

A cage encloses a tank in
which seals perform at this
street fair in Sibley.

6758   JULY 4ᵀᴴ 1910   SHEFFIELD, IOWA

*An Independence Day
parade passes under an arch
spanning the wide, unpaved
Main Street in Sheffield.*

"This is part of the parade
the 4th. The little boys with the
wagon are the 'Miles Savings
Bank' float. Those clowns were
simply great. They were all
Miles boys. Nine of them."

*Boosting America in this
segment of the Independence
Day parade in Slater are Uncle
Sam, a bevy of local belles, and
a float featuring Columbia and
the Liberty Bell.*

*A carousel must have made
the Independence Day celebration
exciting and memorable for the
children of Gaza.*

*Veterans take up arms
once again in observance of
Memorial Day in Denison.*

The photographer took advantage of an unusual vantage point to produce this striking scene of a Memorial Day parade in Mystic.

*County fairs, such as
this one at Waverly in Bremer
County, always were productive
of much boosting and many
postcards.*

Boosting reached a
pinnacle each year in
Des Moines at the week-long
Iowa State Fair, an event well
promoted by postcards, including
many custom-made for those
attending the fair.

6 : Big News

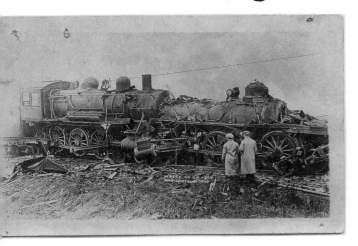

The yen most people have to see true-to-life pictures of persons, places, and events in the news was very far from being satisfied during the first two decades of this century. Because of the costs involved in the half-tone printing process, very few small-town newspapers had the capability of reproducing photographs. Photographic postcards were for a while, in fact, the most common method of transmitting photographic images of local happenings to those outside the immediate area. Possibly this was a major factor accounting for the great postcard craze of that era.

The time required to prepare postcards and get them to customers via the postcard racks of local drugstores was not excessive; in most cases, enterprising photographers could get their postcards onto the racks well within twenty-four hours. Nonetheless, photographic postcards probably always functioned more as souvenirs than as a news medium.

Such recurring events as the annual Sauerkraut Days or Independence Day celebrations were routinely depicted in postcards, but photographers also had to be alert for the local occurrence that went beyond the customary or happened unexpectedly. Scattered throughout the pages of this book are images conveying the flavor of the kinds of small-town news items deemed worthy of being reported in postcards—for example, the laying of a church's cornerstone, the completion of a water tower or of a new railroad line reaching the town, the arrival of the circus or an itinerant revival campaign, or a town's acquisition of a new street-cleaning apparatus.

This chapter presents postcard images representative of two major kinds of "big news" events guaranteed to generate ample postcard coverage: disasters and visits by celebrities. Although campaign stops by candidates for public office must have been the visits most likely to occur, sometimes the governor or other such magnificos might have been on hand to speak on a ceremonial occasion. Visits by politicians and other kinds of celebrities, such as famous aviators, sports figures, and eminent evangelists, were not likely to go unnoticed by postcard photographers. In fact, even virtually unknown visitors might end up on postcards if they were engaged in some novel enterprise, such as crossing the United States by automobile or perhaps on foot or even in a buggy pulled by a team of huskies or wolves.

Disasters were probably chronicled on postcards more often than any other kind of local news event, however—partly because they usually affected or threatened all residents of a town in very major ways, but partly, too, because so many types of disasters could and did occur. The wide scope of possibilities is suggested by the postcards in this chapter, which bear the "big news" of floods, tornadoes, hailstorms, snowstorms, fires, and train wrecks.

R.I. WRECK 2 MI. SO. OF MAYNARD

*Train wrecks always
drew big crowds; at least
half of Maynard's citizens
seem to have turned
out for this one.*

*Scenes of the "wreck
at Rock River" near Doon
adorn this memorial to two
trainmen killed in the
disaster.*

Jones Co. Elevator Burning
Estherville, Ia, July 13, '14.

In Estherville or any other Iowa small town, an elevator fire qualified as big news, definitely worthy of a postcard.

Burning of the Baptist
Church, Vinton, Ia.

BUY ME AND OWN A BRICK
in the
New Baptist Church, Vinton, Ia.

*The Baptists of Vinton
put this photograph of their
misfortune to good use
as a fund-raiser for a
new church building.*

*In addition to empty space
where several businesses had
been, this disastrous fire in
Cedar Falls produced
throngs of gawkers.*

*A scene of rubble near
Arcadia indicates how
devastating the tornadoes
that threaten Iowa every
summer can be.*

A work crew in Sanborn begins the dismal task of cleaning up the debris left in the wake of a tornado.

*A tornado has bestowed on
Jacob Gugger an unobstructed
view of the outdoors, as he sits
in a wheelchair in his house
in Boone.*

*Men wearing hip boots join
children for a wade in a flooded
street in Marengo. But why does
the man on the left also wear
hip boots on his arms?*

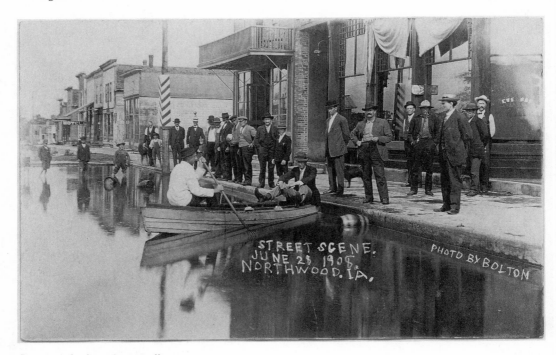

*Because the boat is actually
resting on the street, this photo
makes the flood at Northwood
look worse than it truly was.*

GREETINGS FROM ESTHERVILLE, Iowa. —DIGGING OUT THE SNOW PLOW— FEBRUARY -1909-

The snowplow these men are shoveling out in Estherville was powered by a locomotive and used to clear train tracks.

"This is the good old fashioned winter with much cold weather and lots and lots of snow including sleighrides"— and also hard shoveling, as these men in Sidney know.

CHRISTMAS DAY 1912 IN WEST BRANCH IA.

A Christmas Day on which Iowans could go outside without wearing coats, as in this scene in West Branch, clearly was a newsworthy event.

*Big news from
Rock Falls: this elm tree
"was struck by lightning last
Tuesday morning—ripped
her up in good shape—
3 flashes hit her right
in succession."*

Partial Eclipse of Sun June 19 – 1909
Photo by Zentner Everly Ia.

*Residents of Everly
could prove to the world
that the eclipse did not
bypass their town.*

WRECKING THE CATHOLIC CHURCH AT BELLEVUE IA.

A question left unanswered
is why was this Catholic church
at Bellevue pulled down.

AVIATOR HUGH ROBISON HYDRO AEROPLANE ENROUTE FROM
MINNEAPOLIS TO NEW ORLEANS AT BELLEVUE IA. OCT. 20 1911

A picture of a "hydro aeroplane" landing in Bellevue was certain to be a big seller in the local drugstore's postcard rack.

AT DUBUQUE AVIATION MEET.
LINCOLN BEACHY AND WIFE SIZING UP THE CROWD BEFORE THE FLIGHT.

*An aviation meet in
Dubuque attracted a famous
"early bird" of aviation, Lincoln
Beachy, who not much later
died in a plane crash.*

*Because Iowa was
Republican country, William
Howard Taft got a hearty welcome
when he whistle-stopped in
Mason City during the 1908
presidential campaign.*

*When Klondike Bill,
a colorful transcontinental
itinerant, and his dog team
reached Iowa City, a photographer
snapped them standing next
to the University of Iowa
campus.*

7 : Keeping 'Em Down on the Farm

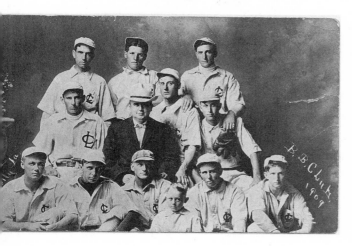

The world of Americans at the start of the century, historian Frederick Lewis Allen notes, was "unbelievably more limited" than the world we now know—a consequence in part of the fact that each town or farm then was "far more dependent upon its own resources" than is true today. That such events as booster days, patriotic celebrations, and county fairs could figure so prominently in the lives (and the photographic postcards) of Iowans bespeaks the truth of Allen's observations. So, too, do some other typical small-town cultural offerings that Iowans recorded on postcards.

The photographic postcard record points to the importance of both school and church in the small-town scheme of things. Then as now, Iowa ranked high among the states in literacy, a reflection of the state's commitment to providing at least a rudimentary education to its citizens. Many postcards showing schools, classrooms, and pupils survive today. The same is true for postcards depicting high school athletic teams; in many of Iowa's small towns, apparently the booster spirit had already begun to find expression in the residents' enthusiastic support of the local school teams, both boys' and girls'. A similar fervor among some Iowans centered on the football teams of Iowa State College (now University) and the University of Iowa, especially during their annual clash on the gridiron.

In addition to being places of worship, churches were focal points for another set of personal relationships and activities of importance in Iowa's small towns. Sunday school outings and church socials and picnics often showed up in photographic postcards, as did revival meetings, another major religious activity.

Iowans, like most other "respectable" Americans of that era, were earnest devotees of the Uplift, which found its most important secular expression in the Chautauqua. This unusual institution, often depicted in Iowa postcards, brought speakers and high-toned events from afar and exposed the residents of small towns to a wider range of notions than they would otherwise ever have known. In spite of its broadening intent and effects, however, Chautauqua was the perfect expression of a provincial mentality and, in and of itself, a good indicator of just how limited were the cultural offerings of the small towns of Iowa.

If Chautauqua and revivals brought outsiders to Iowa towns for the purpose of upgrading the minds and souls of their citizens, others came for the less lofty and more humane purpose of entertaining Iowans. Some of the many circuses then roving America, for instance, were likely to show up in Iowa each summer, always providing subject matter for postcards. A town having an opera house (and many did, as numerous postcards attest) could also expect to be entertained by traveling troupes of actors, musicians, and other vaudeville performers. Only just beginning to be shown here and there in Iowa were motion pictures, which soon would become a major cultural force penetrating the isolated existence of many small towns.

Although few Iowans could afford extensive vacation trips, many were able to get away for brief stays at vacation resorts along the shores of Iowa's larger northern lakes, whence many photographic postcards were sent to envious friends at home. An excursion to an amusement park—another special occasion calling for postcards—was also a summertime entertainment option for those lucky enough to live near a park. For Iowans who had to stay put in their towns or on their farms during the hot summer months—that is, for most Iowans—entertainment was necessarily confined to whatever was brought in or could be produced locally. What that fare might include is illustrated by the first postcard presented in this chapter, "Coming Events in Oskaloosa," which lists the major cultural offerings available to the residents of one small town during a four-week stretch in the summer of 1909.

Oskaloosa was one of many Iowa towns which, responding to the inducements of a special state law, had built bandstands and supported town bands (virtually all of which seem to have been documented in postcards). As a result, Oskaloosa's residents were able to enjoy concerts "every Wednesday and Saturday evenings," as the postcard records. Even more likely to draw big crowds was Buffalo Bill and Pawnee Bill's Big Wild West Show, which was safely sandwiched between two loftier Chautauqua offerings also featuring big-name performers—Billy Sunday and William Jennings Bryan. Giving the most promise of sustained excitement, however, was the "Big Labor Day Celebration"; this three-day blowout, which doubtless began with a parade, included an Old Settlers' reunion and another booster event called "Home-Coming of the Mahaskans" and was accented by three evening performances of "Pain's Big Fire Spectacles," a pyrotechnical extravaganza "costing $3,000."

These were public or commercial events, but the residents of Oskaloosa—indeed, every town in the state—also had open to them a multitude of self-generated, informal, small-group activities, such as swimming, fishing, camping, picnicking, playing cards or croquet, producing amateur theatricals, or simply chatting with friends. Small-town folks today continue to enjoy these things, of course, but at the dawn of this century such activities necessarily filled a much larger place in the lives of Iowans. The fact is confirmed, perhaps, by the large number and great variety of simple pleasures which Iowans thought worthy of being memorialized in photographic postcards. The great appeal which these postcards have is evident in the few examples included in this chapter.

The impression conveyed by the postcard record unquestionably is of a small-town existence which was much more limited and which imposed many more restrictions than most Americans of the late twentieth century probably could bear. At the same time, however, it is undeniable that the Iowans shown in these postcards seem content, even happy. Moreover, the things they are shown doing suggest that it was an era which can be characterized accurately, in historian Richard Hofstadter's felicitous phrase, as one of "innocent relaxation." This quality, which soon departed forever from American life, is likely to spark a modicum of envy among many Iowans and other Americans today.

Statue of Chief Mahaska in Public Park, Oskaloosa. Dedicated May 12, 1909.

WEST SIDE SQUARE
ESTABLISHED 1861
OLD RELIABLE :

Coming Events in Oskaloosa.

Band Concert in Park every Wednesday and Saturday evenings.

AUG. 9-14—Our Special Sale of China and Cut Glass, Half Price.

AUG. 11—Billy Sunday at Chautauqua, 2:30 p. m.

AUG. 14—Buffalo Bill and Pawnee Bill's Big Wild West Show.

AUG. 14 Farmers' Day at the Chautauqua.

AUG. 16-21—Our Special Sale, Rings, Half Price.

AUG. 17—Wm. J. Bryan at Chautauqua, 8:00 p. m.

AUG. 23-28—Our Special Sale, Clocks and Brassware, Half Price.

AUG 30—Iowa Yearly Meeting of Friends, commences, closes Sept. 6

AUG 30-SEPT. 4—Our Special Sale, Watches, all kinds, sizes and prices, Half Price.

SEPT. 6—Big Labor Day Celebration, under auspices Oskaloosa Trades Assembly.

SEPT. 7—Annual Meeting of the Mahaska County Old Settlers' Association

SEPT. 8—"Home-Coming of the Mahaskans "

Monday, Tuesday and Wednesday Nights SEPT. 6-7-8—Pain's Big Fire Spectacles at the Oskaloosa Ball Park, costing $3,000.

SEPT. 8-9-10—Reunion of the Thirty-third Iowa Infantry.

SEPT. 13-18—Last week of our Celebrated Stock Closing Out Sale, including all remaining stock,

SEPT. 13-14—Colleges Open.

COMPLIMENTS OF

T. K. Smith Jewelry House

MANUFACTURING JEWELERS   R. R. WATCH INSPECTORS

OSKALOOSA -   -   -   -   -   IOWA

End-of-the-summer events like these in Oskaloosa could be found in many small towns throughout Iowa.

In Ida Grove, as in any other Iowa small town, a circus always began with a big parade.

*A circus brought a taste of
an exotic world lying beyond
the confines of an Iowa town—
in this case, Boone.*

*Fantana probably
offered its "clean" and
"refined" "tableau de art"
at a fair or amusement
park somewhere near
Davenport.*

In the summer, band
concerts were a major
entertainment in Iowa towns,
which often put up handsome
bandstands, such as this
one in What Cheer.

Many towns sponsored
bands, but surely none was
more spiffily clad than the
Guthrie Center military
band.

In spite of the hifalutin
name, opera houses in Iowa
small towns were often no more
imposing or elegant than this
one in Farnhamville.

"How do you like the looks of Camanchie's [sic] new Dramatic Club?"—and of a theater plastered with advertisements by local merchants?

*In Grundy Center, the Gem
movie theater is ready to offer
a double feature.*

*Any self-respecting town,
such as Webster City, had
a baseball park, which also
happened to be another good
site for advertisements.*

Photographic postcards from many places besides Lohrville indicate that croquet was a very popular game in Iowa.

From Grundy Center comes this cliché image of the "good old days" before farm chemical runoffs had polluted the "ol' swimmin' hole."

At Lake View, friends or
perhaps an extended family (is
that Grandpa in the hammock
on the left?) take a holiday
in cottages near Black
Hawk Lake.

*Even on a lakeside vacation
at Arnolds Park on Lake Okoboji,
norms of prim and proper dress
prevailed.*

Ready for a Swim,
Clear Lake, Iowa.

*A swim in Clear Lake must
have been an ordeal once those
swimsuits were water-soaked.*

*A young man drinks in the
wisdom on tap from four sages
who have gathered for a palaver
at Moses' Store in Keota.*

*On a picnic near Ogden,
the men have slipped away for
a card game (doubtless leaving
the women to prepare or
clean up after the meal).*

*At Cedar and virtually all
other towns in Iowa, classroom
photographs of pupils in the
local schools were standard
fare for postcards.*

The juxtaposition of a massive
school building and small figures
of pupils and teachers produces
an impressive image on this
postcard from Dayton.

*College-bound graduates of
Vail High School are honored
at a ceremony whose theme is
"Impossible Is Unamerican." But
why are the two small girls in
swings there?*

BASKET BALL GAME CHILDRENS DAY ALVORD IA.

Vigorous human activity and pastoral serenity are skillfully joined to compose this wonderful photographic souvenir of a special communal event in Alvord.

This picture of the girls' basketball team of Manning High School reveals that the girls' game played in Iowa did not always require six players.

Four years we served
in our high school
Four years we've served
And never broke a rule.
We all played foot-ball
But none of us are cruel
We are the merry seniors
of our High School.

Although postcards depicting Iowa high school sports teams are commonplace, dithyrambic embellishments make this one from Clarion special.

*In Iowa City, the Cyclones
and the Hawkeyes clash on the
gridiron; postcards probably sold
well each year to alumni and
students on the winning side.*

A message on a companion
card reads: "This is a picture
of part of the annual push-ball
game between sophomores and
freshmen [at Iowa State College
in Ames]. Everything is allowed
in it from kicking each other's
shins to murder in the third
degree."

*"We had a fine Chautauqua
in Colo. This is a picture of the
crowd taken on an afternoon. . . .
We had a week of it. . . . We took
it all in. I never missed but one."*

*These young women tenting
on the Chautauqua grounds at
Columbus Junction remain under
the watchful eye of a chaperone,
Mrs. Stone.*

Elbert Hubbard
Will give his Lecture
"Health and Wealth"
(Auspices of The Universal Chiropractors'
Association)
In the

P. S. C. Auditorium
DAVENPORT, IOWA

FRIDAY EVENING
August 28th, 1914
at Eight o'Clock
Price of Admission, Fifty Cents
Reserved seats on sale at Nabstedt's
Jewelry Store

*Elbert Hubbard, a gifted
self-promoter, addressed this
classic American topic in the
Davenport precincts of his
pal of chiropractic fame,
B. J. Palmer.*

When much of
small-town social
and cultural life centered
on fraternal organizations,
a parade at Shenandoah
featuring brother Elks
could draw a big
crowd.

"Dear Mr. and Mrs. Williams:
Be sure and come up to church
[in Brooklyn] next Sunday, June 21.
We will dedicate the new building
and have a basket dinner. Don't
miss it. Be here in time for S.S.
[Sunday school]. From Bro.
Knoles."

*No rain spoiled this
big day for the Methodists
of Shenandoah, but umbrellas
and parasols were needed to
protect against the sun.*

*Even during the
photo session of this
Sunday school outing in
Pleasant Hill the teacher
keeps his eyes fixed on
the Bible.*

*These members of
a Sunday school baseball
team in Reasnor look about
as old as their teacher (also
coach?).*

Preaching the funeral of R C Coopers

*Photographs of funerals are
seldom as pleasing to the eye
as this one from Drakesville.*

*"This is the evangelist
holding meetings—on the
3d week [in Victor]. We like
him fine." Apparently, young
men were his special quarry.*

*"Billy Sunday on chair
holding flag during famous
booze sermon." The most famous
evangelist of the day whoops
it up in Marshalltown.*

HELL: And How to Get there
Subject Sunday Evening October 16th

HELL: And who will be there
Subject for Sunday Evening October 23rd

TIME—7:30

PLACE—CALVARY BAPTIST CHURCH
Corner 5th Ave and 6th St. West

Preacher: Rev. John Hastie

Come And Bring Some One With You Come

Cedar Rapids was treated
to yet another harangue on
one of the favorite themes of
evangelists, then and now.

8 : 'Til the Boys Come Home

World War I may not have lived up to its billing as the war to end all wars, but it did play a major part in bringing to an end the world depicted in the postcards in this book. "Almost overnight," according to historian Walter Lord, "Americans lost a happy, easy-going, confident way of looking at things." In the judgment of another historian, Henry F. May, the Great War marked the end of "American innocence" and also of the previous "Victorian calm."

A grisly, sobering event, World War I not only marked the end of an era but was also the start of a succession of crises, calamities, and changes disturbing the tranquillity of Americans ever since. The nation's participation in the war foretold, too, a new and dangerous relationship with the rest of the world, one which Americans in not many more years were forced to accept as unavoidable and permanent. With the war's end also came a hastened pace of life, while at the same time the country became embroiled in new cultural conflicts and changes on a large scale. "Keeping 'em down on the farm" became increasingly difficult to do, as a popular song of that day acknowledged.

Although President Harding pledged his administration to the "return to normalcy," that objective lay beyond the possibility of permanent realization. Yet the broad popular support for the president's vision of a restored prewar America indicates that most Americans neither favored a departure from their prewar world nor doubted that it could be perpetuated in the postwar era. Indeed, from the start the vast majority of Americans probably never had the slightest inkling that the war might be a grave threat to their familiar world. Hence, America's entry into the war in 1917 brought forth an unreserved outpouring of patriotic fervor. Soon this mighty force was channelled into a finely orchestrated national effort to recruit soldiers and sailors, sell war bonds, whip up war sentiment, search out spies, harass German Americans, and jail various "undesirables" on charges of sedition.

Among the millions of noncombatant Americans enlisting in this noble enterprise were photographers, who captured some aspects of the great patriotic crusade in postcards. This chapter presents several postcards recording events on the home front in Iowa—such things as bond drives, troop train departures, patriotic parades, and Armistice Day celebrations. A striking characteristic of the images in these postcards is their depiction of large masses of people. In this respect they hint at a major truth about the war: it was a great collective undertaking in whose service all Americans were expected to enlist and to which all individual interests were to be subordinated.

But also included here are a few examples of another, sharply contrasting kind of photographic postcard prominent during the war years. These postcards portrayed, usually singly but sometimes in pairs or other small groupings, the doughboys and sailors called up from the small towns and farms of Iowa. These are the more engaging of the wartime postcards, because they bring us face to face with those who shouldered the real burden of the war. Their portraits are rendered all the more poignant by the realization that some of these young Iowans didn't make it through the war and very likely died believing they were defending the Iowa and the America they had always known. Those who did return, however, as well as all who had remained on the home front, soon saw their familiar world steadily assailed by change and pushed inexorably toward transformation.

Another casualty of the war was the postcard craze, which had already begun to subside as early as 1914. Although photographic postcards continued to be made after the war years (into the 1950s, in fact), their heyday was over. The brief "golden age" of photographic postcards left a rich legacy, however, providing us today with an abundance of vivid and engaging glimpses of Iowa in the opening decades of the twentieth century. And while a few readers may demur, probably most will readily agree that the selection of glimpses offered here also depicts an Iowa standing at a far remove—one measured not just in years—from the Iowa which will soon take its turn at opening a new century.

CRSON CO. IOWA BOYS MAY 10-1918 - CUNDILL PHOTO.

Posing for this group
photo on the steps of the
courthouse in Maquoketa,
these fresh-faced Iowa youths
have just been processed
for the draft (note tags
on lapels).

At the train depot in Marengo, well-wishers bid farewell to Iowa County soldiers going off to fight the heathen Hun.

This and the next three studio shots show Iowa lads called up for the great crusade against the Kaiser.

*In front of the post office
in Hawarden, Iowans are
squeezed for money in
a Liberty Loan drive.*

On the home front, churches
gave their blessings to the war
effort, as in this float in a
parade in Waterloo.

Residents take to the streets
of Avoca to celebrate Germany's
surrender and the war's end.

No doubt Camp Dodge supplied the soldiers marching down Locust Street in Des Moines in this Armistice Day celebration in 1918.

*In Tama and elsewhere in
the U.S., Johnnie came marching
home again to a postwar world
that would rapidly diverge from
the one he had left.*

References

For historical background information and all direct quotations in this book, I drew upon the following: Frederick Lewis Allen, *The Big Change: America Transforms Itself, 1900–1950,* Harper and Brothers, 1952; Richard Hofstadter, *The Age of Reform: From Bryan to F.D.R.,* Knopf, 1955; John A. Jakle, *The American Small Town: Twentieth-Century Place Images,* Archon Books, 1982; Walter Lord, *The Good Years: From 1900 to the First World War,* Harper and Brothers, 1960; Henry F. May, *The End of American Innocence,* Knopf, 1959; and Joseph F. Wall, *Iowa: A Bicentennial History,* W. W. Norton, 1978. Most of the statistical data about Iowa I got from this last book and from the 1905 *Census of Iowa.*

For information about early photographic postcards, I consulted the following: the introductory essay in H. Roger Grant, *Railroad Postcards in the Age of Steam,* University of Iowa Press, 1994; Deborah Lengkeek, ed., *Postcard Collector Annual: Commemorating 100 Years of the Postcard,* Jones Publishing (Iola, Wisconsin), 1993; George Miller and Dorothy Miller, *Picture Postcards in the U.S., 1893–1918,* Crown, 1975; and Hal Morgan and Andreas Brown, *Prairie Fires and Paper Moons: The American Photographic Postcard: 1900–1920,* David R. Godine, 1981.

Index of Towns

Ackley, 160
Adair, 10
Akron, 102
Albia, 115
Algona, 35
Alton, 98
Alvord, 219
Ames, 20, 223
Arcadia, 180
Arnold's Park, 212
Atlantic, 16
Avoca, 248

Bellevue, 26, 190, 191
Berlin (Lincoln), 84
Bethlehem, 128
Boone, 56, 85, 182, 201
Bradford, 125
Brooklyn, 228
Buxton, 88, 148

Camanche, 206
Casey, 123
Cedar, 216
Cedar Falls, 179
Cedar Rapids, 142, 235
Cherokee, 54, 158

Clarion, 221
Clarksville, 53
Clear Lake, 213
Clinton, v
Coggon, 86
Colo, 45, 224
Columbus Junction, 225
Cone (Conesville), 159
Conesville (Cone), 159

Davenport, 144, 202, 226
Dawson, 97
Dayton, 217
Denison, 168
Des Moines, 29, 51, 94, 119, 132, 133, 171, 249
Doon, 176
Drakesville, 232
Dubuque, 192
Dyersville, 153

Eddyville, 134
Ellsworth, 79
Elmira, 95
Essex, 55
Estherville, 177, 185
Everly, 189

Farnhamville, 205
Fern, 66
Fonda, 106
Fort Madison, 40, 135

Garner, 13
Garwin, 121
Gaza, 167
Glenwood, 68
Goodell, 124
Gowrie, 1, 129
Grundy Center, 207, 210
Guthrie Center, 204

Haverhill, 137
Hawarden, 246
Herndon, 138
Hocking, 122
Homestead, 141

Ida Grove, 131, 200
Iowa City, 104, 109, 194, 222

Jefferson, 76, 173

Keota, 152, 214

Lake City, 195
Lake View, 211
Latimer, 156

Lenox, 126, 162
Lincoln (Berlin), 84
Lohrville, 209
Lucas, 147

Manning, 220
Maquoketa, 154, 155, 240
Marengo, 30, 183, 241
Marion, 78
Marshalltown, 41, 234
Mason City, 60, 64, 92, 110, 193
Maynard, 175
Miles, 165
Missouri Valley, 251
Muscatine, 21, 145
Mystic, 169

National, 10
New Hampton, 100
New Sharon, 17, 37
Northwood, 184

Oelwein, 113
Ogden, 215
Osceola, 33, 44, 140, 199
Oskaloosa, 8, 28
Oxford Junction, 19, 34, 43

Paullina, 75
Plainfield, 67

Pleasant Hill, 230
Pocahontas, 24
Pomeroy, 25
Prescott, 105

Quasqueton, 107

Ralston, 59
Reasnor, 231
Reinbeck, iii, 39
Richland, 12
Rochester, 157
Rock Falls, 188
Rubio, 87

Sanborn, 181
Sandyville, 70
Sheffield, 164
Shelby, 42
Shenandoah, 52, 103, 227, 229
Sibley, 163
Sidney, 89, 186
Sioux City, 22, 111
Sioux Rapids, 27, 127

Slater, 91, 166
Springville, 57
Stanhope, 136
State Center, 112
Stratford, 11, 61

Tama, 32, 250
Traer, 90

Vail, 161, 218
Victor, 139, 233
Vinton, 178

Walcott, 74
Wapello, 38
Ward, 96
Washington, 36
Waterloo, 62, 63, 65, 130, 247
Waverly, vii, 64, 93, 170
Webster City, 120, 208
Wellman, 108
West Branch, 187
West Liberty, 143
What Cheer, 99, 146, 203

Selected Bur Oak Books

"All Will Yet Be Well": The Diary of Sarah
Gillespie Huftalen, 1873–1952
    By Suzanne L. Bunkers
A Cook's Tour of Iowa
    By Susan Puckett
A Country So Full of Game:
The Story of Wildlife in Iowa
    By James J. Dinsmore
The Des Moines Register Cookbook
    *By Carol McGarvey, Marie McCartan, and
    C. R. Mitchell*
The Folks
    By Ruth Suckow
An Iowa Album:
A Photographic History, 1860–1920
    By Mary Bennett
More han Ola og han Per
    By Peter J. Rosendahl
Neighboring on the Air:
Cooking with the KMA Radio Homemakers
    By Evelyn Birkby
Nineteenth Century Home Architecture of Iowa
City: A Silver Anniversary Edition
    By Margaret N. Keyes
Nothing to Do but Stay: My Pioneer Mother
    By Carrie Young
Old Capitol: Portrait of an Iowa Landmark
    By Margaret N. Keyes
Parsnips in the Snow:
Talks with Midwestern Gardeners
    By Jane Anne Staw and Mary Swander

A Place of Sense:
Essays in Search of the Midwest
    Edited by Michael Martone
Prairie Cooks: Glorified Rice, Three-Day
Buns, and Other Reminiscences
    By Carrie Young with Felicia Young
A Ruth Suckow Omnibus
    By Ruth Suckow
"A Secret to Be Burried": The Diary and Life
of Emily Hawley Gillespie, 1858–1888
    By Judy Nolte Lensink
Tales of an Old Horsetrader:
The First Hundred Years
    By Leroy Judson Daniels
The Tattooed Countess
    By Carl Van Vechten
"This State of Wonders": The Letters of
an Iowa Frontier Family, 1858–1861
    Edited by John Kent Folmar
Townships
    Edited by Michael Martone
Up a Country Lane Cookbook
    By Evelyn Birkby
Vandemark's Folly
    By Herbert Quick
The Wedding Dress:
Stories from the Dakota Plains
    By Carrie Young